The History

Enchanted Pagodas and Empires Lost

The contents of this book are intended for entertainment purposes only. While every effort has been made to ensure the accuracy and reliability of the information presented, the author and publisher make no warranties or representations as to the accuracy, completeness, or suitability of the information contained herein. The information presented in this book is not intended as a substitute for professional advice, and readers should consult with qualified professionals in the relevant fields for specific advice.

Land of Legends: Mythical Origins and Early Settlers

In the shadowy corridors of time, Myanmar's history is woven with the threads of mythology and the footprints of early settlers. Nestled in the lush landscapes of Southeast Asia, this ancient land has been shaped by both legendary tales and tangible evidence of human presence.

Mythical origins cast a captivating veil over Myanmar's beginnings. According to local legends, the land was once ruled by powerful beings known as "Nats," supernatural spirits that held sway over the elements and fate. Mount Popa, a towering volcanic peak, was believed to be the dwelling place of these Nats, attracting pilgrims seeking divine blessings.

Long before recorded history, the region's fertile plains and river valleys beckoned early settlers. Archaeological evidence traces human habitation back to the Paleolithic era, with artifacts such as stone tools and cave paintings discovered in various sites. As the millennia unfolded, the intricate dance of migration and cultural exchange shaped Myanmar's identity.

The Neolithic period brought about significant changes, with agricultural practices taking root. Communities transitioned from hunter-gatherer lifestyles to settled farming, cultivating crops like rice, millet, and beans. This shift laid the foundation for more organized societies and the emergence of distinct cultures.

By the 3rd century BCE, the Pyu city-states were flourishing, forming the first known urban centers in Myanmar. The city of Sri Ksetra, with its well-planned layout and sophisticated infrastructure, stood as a testament to the Pyu's advanced civilization. The people engaged in trade, connecting Myanmar to neighboring lands and fostering cultural exchanges that enriched their way of life.

As time progressed, the Mon people left an indelible mark on Myanmar's early history. Establishing city-states like Thaton, they engaged in maritime trade that linked them with Indian and Southeast Asian civilizations. It was during this period that Theravada Buddhism gained prominence, bringing with it a spiritual and architectural legacy that would leave an enduring impact.

The Bamar people, who would go on to establish the Pagan Dynasty, arrived in the region around the 9th century CE. With their ascent, a new chapter in Myanmar's history was written. The city of Pagan (modern-day Bagan) flourished as the capital, adorned with thousands of stupas, temples, and monasteries. This architectural marvel showcased the Bamar's devotion to Buddhism and their mastery of artistic craftsmanship.

As time weaves its intricate tapestry, the mythic origins and early settlers of Myanmar continue to resonate in the layers of history. The land's foundation was forged by the convergence of myth and reality, as legendary Nats watched over its landscapes and pioneering settlers shaped its destiny. This chapter unveils the enigmatic beginnings of a nation, setting the stage for the rich tapestry of events and cultures that would follow.

Pyu Kingdoms: Flourishing Civilizations of Ancient Myanmar

In the heart of ancient Myanmar, a tapestry of flourishing civilizations unfolded with the rise of the Pyu Kingdoms. Situated in the central and northern regions of the country, these kingdoms would become centers of trade, culture, and innovation, leaving an indelible mark on Myanmar's historical landscape.

The Pyu Kingdoms emerged as early as the 2nd century BCE and reached their zenith between the 4th and 9th centuries CE. Their territories stretched across the fertile plains of modern-day central Myanmar, with cities like Sri Ksetra, Halin, and Beikthano serving as epicenters of Pyu culture and governance.

Sri Ksetra, also known as Thaye Khittaya, stood as the crowning jewel of Pyu urban planning and architectural prowess. The city's strategic location near the Irrawaddy River facilitated trade and cultural exchanges with distant lands, including India, China, and Southeast Asia. With its well-organized layout, fortified walls, and grand religious monuments, Sri Ksetra embodied the Pyu's sophisticated understanding of urban development.

Trade played a pivotal role in the Pyu Kingdoms' prosperity. Their strategic position along the Southern Silk Road and the maritime trade routes facilitated the exchange of goods, ideas, and cultural influences. This exposure fostered a diverse tapestry of artistic expression, as seen in the intricate carvings, pottery, and jewelry that have been unearthed from archaeological sites.

Buddhism, introduced by early Indian traders and missionaries, took root within the Pyu Kingdoms. The construction of stupas, monasteries, and Buddhist sculptures reflected the Pyu people's devotion to their faith and their skilled craftsmanship. The influence of Theravada Buddhism intertwined with local beliefs, creating a unique syncretic spiritual landscape.

The Pyu script, known as the Pyu language or Pyu script, was a written form of communication used by these ancient societies. Evidence of this script can be found on inscriptions, artifacts, and coins, shedding light on their administrative systems, religious practices, and cultural achievements.

Halin and Beikthano, other notable Pyu cities, added to the richness of this civilization. Halin, with its distinct circular fortifications and city layout, revealed the Pyu's adeptness in urban planning. Beikthano, nestled near present-day Taungoo, featured remnants of moats and palace structures, showcasing the Pyu's intricate architectural techniques.

The Pyu Kingdoms' prominence gradually waned, giving way to the rise of the Bamar Empire in the central region of Myanmar. Nevertheless, their legacy persisted in the cultural mosaic of the nation. The Pyu's contributions to urban planning, trade, religion, and art continue to resonate in Myanmar's historical narrative.

Mon Dynasties: Coastal Influences and Maritime Trade

Along the picturesque coastlines of ancient Myanmar, a maritime saga unfolded as the Mon Dynasties rose to power. Carved by the waves of history and the interplay of coastal cultures, these dynasties left an indelible mark on Myanmar's historical narrative through their unique blend of trade, art, and governance.

The Mon people, with their roots in Southeast Asia, established their presence in the coastal areas of present-day Myanmar well before the Common Era. Known for their seafaring skills, the Mon's connection to maritime trade and cultural exchanges became the cornerstone of their influence.

The earliest recorded Mon Dynasty, the Dvaravati Kingdom, flourished in the region from the 6th to the 11th centuries CE. Situated in the lower Irrawaddy Delta, the kingdom's proximity to the sea enabled thriving trade with India, Sri Lanka, and other Southeast Asian realms. This maritime network facilitated the exchange of goods such as textiles, spices, precious gems, and ivory.

The Mon people's skillful navigation of the sea routes contributed to their cosmopolitan outlook. This is exemplified by the Kingdom of Thaton, a coastal city-state that stood as a vibrant cultural crossroads. Its proximity to the Bay of Bengal allowed Thaton to serve as a vital link between the Indian subcontinent and Southeast Asia. The city's wealth and influence were reflected in its golden pagodas, bustling markets, and learned monastic institutions. The influence of Indian culture on the Mon Dynasties was particularly noteworthy. With the arrival of Indian traders, the Mon people embraced Theravada Buddhism and became fervent patrons of religious art and architecture. The colossal Shwedagon Pagoda in Yangon, initially built by the Mon and later enriched by successive generations, stands as a testament to their devotion and artistic finesse.

Mon script, a written language derived from Indian scripts, became the conduit for recording religious texts and historical accounts. This script, adorned with ornate calligraphy, was inscribed on palm leaves and preserved in monastic libraries. Mon script's legacy endures through the inscriptional records that offer insights into the dynasties' governance and religious practices.

As Myanmar's history unfolded, the Mon Dynasties faced a series of challenges, including conflicts with neighboring powers like the Bamar and the Khmer. However, their cultural legacy persisted and was absorbed into the fabric of the nation. The Mon's artistic contributions, from intricate wood carvings to ornate temple decorations, continue to shape Myanmar's cultural identity.

The Mon Dynasties, with their maritime prowess and vibrant coastal cities, stand as a testament to the interplay between geography, culture, and history. Their legacy is woven into the architectural marvels, artistic treasures, and cultural diversity that characterize Myanmar's narrative. Through their maritime trade networks and cross-cultural interactions, the Mon people forged a path that echoes through time, leaving behind a legacy of rich heritage and enduring influence.

Bamar Empire Emergence: Pagan Dynasty's Rise to Power

Amidst the ancient landscapes of Myanmar, a transformative chapter in its history unfolded with the emergence of the Bamar Empire, marked by the rise of the Pagan Dynasty. This period witnessed the ascendancy of a powerful empire that would leave an indelible mark on Myanmar's cultural and historical landscape.

The Bamar people, an ethnic group with origins in the Tibetan-Burman region, migrated southward into the central plains of Myanmar in the 9th century CE. It was during this time that King Anawrahta, a visionary monarch, ascended the throne. He is often credited with laying the foundation for the Pagan Dynasty's rise to power.

Anawrahta's reign marked a turning point in Myanmar's history. His conversion to Theravada Buddhism led to significant cultural and religious shifts, as the king and his court embraced the faith fervently. Inspired by his devotion, Anawrahta embarked on a mission to unify and centralize the region under his rule, ushering in an era of political consolidation. One of Anawrahta's most iconic achievements was the construction of temples and pagodas, notably the Ananda Temple, which stands as a testament to the Pagan Dynasty's architectural prowess. The temple's symmetrical design, exquisite murals, and spiritual significance showcased the dynasty's dedication to Buddhism and its impact on the arts.

The Pagan Dynasty's ascendancy was characterized by its strategic alliances and conquests. Anawrahta's successors continued his legacy, expanding the empire's borders through military campaigns and diplomatic negotiations. The dynasty's reach extended beyond its heartland to encompass a vast expanse of territory, including parts of present-day Thailand and Cambodia.

Trade flourished under Pagan rule, connecting the empire to distant lands through land and maritime routes. The flow of goods, including spices, textiles, and precious metals, enriched the empire and fostered cultural exchanges with neighboring regions. Pagan's position as a cultural crossroads further solidified its influence on the region.

Religious texts and historical records were meticulously preserved during this era. The Tripitaka, the Theravada Buddhist scriptures, were inscribed on palm leaves and stored in pagoda libraries, safeguarding the spiritual knowledge and teachings of the time. These texts offer insights into the religious practices, governance, and daily life of the Pagan Dynasty.

The Pagan Dynasty's dominance eventually waned, partly due to external pressures such as Mongol invasions. However, its legacy continued to influence Myanmar's trajectory. The temples and pagodas that still grace the Bagan landscape serve as living reminders of the dynasty's cultural and architectural contributions.

The emergence of the Bamar Empire and the rise of the Pagan Dynasty cast a transformative shadow on Myanmar's history. Through visionary leadership, religious devotion, and cultural patronage, the dynasty left an enduring legacy that continues to shape the nation's identity and narrative. The Pagan Dynasty's legacy stands as a testament to the resilience and innovation of Myanmar's past, contributing to the intricate mosaic of its historical journey.

Temples of Bagan: Architectural Marvels and Spiritual Centers

Within the sun-kissed plains of Myanmar lies a mesmerizing panorama of architectural splendor and spiritual significance—the temples of Bagan. These timeless monuments stand as a testament to the artistic ingenuity, religious devotion, and cultural richness of an era long past.

The Pagan Dynasty's reign from the 9th to the 13th centuries witnessed the construction of over 10,000 temples, stupas, and monasteries across the Bagan landscape. These architectural marvels emerged as symbols of the dynasty's power, the people's faith, and the convergence of artistic excellence.

The temples vary in scale and design, reflecting the evolving architectural styles and the dynastic shifts that marked their construction. The early temples, such as the Shwezigon Pagoda, are characterized by their simplicity and harmony with the surrounding landscape. As the dynasty progressed, temples like the Ananda Temple and Dhammayangyi Pagoda showcased more intricate designs, featuring ornate carvings, towering spires, and detailed frescoes.

The Ananda Temple, often considered a masterpiece of Bagan architecture, harmoniously blends Indian and Mon influences. Its symmetrical layout, distinctive Buddha images, and exquisite glazed tiles exhibit the artistic finesse of the time. The Dhammayangyi Pagoda, with its massive dimensions and solid brickwork, stands as a testament to King Narathu's ambitious vision.

These temples were not only architectural wonders but also centers of spiritual devotion and learning. Monastic complexes like the Shwezigon Pagoda provided a space for meditation, study, and religious contemplation. The frescoes adorning the walls of temples such as the Sulamani Temple offered narratives from Buddhist texts, transforming the spaces into visual libraries of religious stories.

The Bagan temples also played a pivotal role in the spread of Theravada Buddhism. Monks from India, Sri Lanka, and other regions converged at Bagan, fostering an exchange of ideas and spiritual teachings. The presence of these monks added depth to the religious and intellectual life of the dynasty.

The temples' construction techniques were as varied as their designs. The use of fired bricks and lime mortar allowed for durability, while the sophisticated arrangement of vaults and domes showcased the architectural advancements of the time. Some temples were adorned with stucco decorations and intricate wood carvings, demonstrating the mastery of multiple crafts.

The Bagan temples' journey through time has been marked by challenges, including earthquakes and centuries of weathering. Despite these trials, preservation efforts continue to safeguard these treasures. The temples remain active places of worship, drawing both locals and visitors to experience their spiritual ambiance and architectural grandeur.

Mrauk U: Splendor of the Arakan Empire

In the western reaches of Myanmar lies a hidden gem of history and architectural marvels—the ancient city of Mrauk U. Nestled amidst rolling hills and verdant landscapes, Mrauk U stands as a testament to the grandeur and cultural richness of the Arakan Empire.

The Arakan Empire, also known as the Kingdom of Mrauk U, flourished from the 15th to the 18th centuries CE. Its strategic location along major trade routes and maritime connections fostered a vibrant exchange of goods and ideas, contributing to its opulence and cosmopolitan character.

Mrauk U's rise to prominence was closely linked to its maritime prowess. Its strategic position along the Bay of Bengal allowed it to engage in maritime trade with neighboring empires, such as Bengal, India, and Southeast Asia. The bustling port city became a hub of commerce, attracting merchants, scholars, and travelers from far and wide.

The architecture of Mrauk U is a captivating fusion of local traditions and external influences. The temples, stupas, and palaces that adorn the landscape reflect a blend of Indian, Southeast Asian, and local Arakanese styles. Structures like the Shittaung Pagoda, boasting intricate stone carvings and a maze of passages, highlight the city's artistic achievements.

One of Mrauk U's most iconic structures is the Htukkanthein Temple, renowned for its fortress-like appearance and intricate stucco decorations. The temple's central chamber houses a colossal seated Buddha, while its interior walls are adorned with intricate reliefs depicting scenes from Buddhist tales and Arakanese history.

Mrauk U was not only a center of architectural brilliance but also a hub of religious scholarship and cultural exchange. Buddhist monasteries like the Koe Thaung Temple served as centers of learning and spiritual practice, attracting scholars and monks from across the region. The city's libraries preserved a wealth of religious texts and historical records.

The Arakan Empire's decline was marked by internal conflicts and external pressures, including invasions by the Mughal Empire. By the 18th century, Mrauk U's influence waned, and the city fell into relative obscurity. Despite the passage of time, the remnants of this once-great empire continue to captivate and inspire.

Modern preservation efforts seek to safeguard Mrauk U's heritage. The city's archaeological sites, temples, and artifacts are a testament to the dedication of scholars, historians, and local communities in preserving the legacy of the Arakan Empire.

Mrauk U stands as a window into a glorious chapter of Myanmar's history. Its architectural splendor, cultural exchanges, and maritime prowess shaped the character of the Arakan Empire. As travelers and historians explore its ruins and monuments, they uncover a world of elegance, grandeur, and cultural fusion—a world that has left an indelible mark on Myanmar's historical tapestry.

Shan States and the Mongol Invasion

In the intricate mosaic of Myanmar's history, the Shan States emerged as a dynamic and diverse collection of territories, each with its own cultural nuances and political aspirations. This chapter unravels the tale of these states, their interactions, and the tumultuous epoch of the Mongol invasion that left an indelible mark on the region.

The Shan States, nestled in the eastern highlands of Myanmar, were a constellation of polities with distinct ethnic identities and ruling dynasties. Governed by Sawbwas, local chieftains, these states exhibited a mix of autonomy and allegiance to larger empires that dominated Myanmar's landscape.

The Shan States' history intertwines with that of the Bamar and other surrounding empires. They were renowned for their trade networks, linking Myanmar to China, Thailand, and other Southeast Asian regions. This trade facilitated cultural exchanges and contributed to the vibrant diversity of the Shan States.

The 13th century marked a pivotal juncture with the Mongol invasion looming on the horizon. Led by Kublai Khan, the Mongols sought to expand their empire, and Myanmar's rich territories were within their sights. In 1277, King Narathihapate of the Pagan Dynasty attempted to assert his authority over the Shan States, only to be met with resistance from the Shan rulers.

The Mongol invasion, which followed in 1287, marked a turning point in Myanmar's history. King Narathihapate's forces were overwhelmed by the Mongol army's superior tactics and strategies. Pagan, the heartland of Myanmar's culture and history, fell to the Mongols, leading to the disintegration of the Pagan Dynasty's rule.

The Mongol invasion sparked a period of political fragmentation and reshuffling of power. The Shan States, in particular, emerged as key players in this complex landscape. Some states submitted to Mongol rule, while others retained their autonomy under Shan leaders. The Mongol influence in Myanmar was ephemeral, as the empire soon faced internal strife and other pressing concerns.

The Mongol invasion had lasting repercussions on Myanmar's political and cultural trajectory. The vacuum left by the fall of Pagan was gradually filled by new power centers, including the Shan States and the Toungoo Dynasty. The Mongol threat also left a sense of vulnerability that influenced subsequent dynasties' policies toward foreign powers.

The legacy of the Shan States and the Mongol invasion continues to shape Myanmar's historical narrative. The Shan States' unique identities and historical experiences contribute to the country's rich cultural mosaic. Meanwhile, the Mongol invasion remains a cautionary tale of the impermanence of power and the complex interactions that have defined Myanmar's journey through time.

Arrival of the Europeans: Colonial Struggles and Shifting Power

In the annals of Myanmar's history, a new chapter unfolded with the arrival of European powers on its shores. The 16th to 19th centuries witnessed a complex interplay of colonial ambitions, shifting alliances, and struggles for supremacy that left an indelible mark on the country's trajectory.

The European arrival marked a departure from the region's earlier interactions with neighboring empires. Portuguese explorers were among the first to establish contact, followed by the Dutch, French, and British. These powers were driven by economic interests, including the lucrative spice trade and access to Asian markets.

The Portuguese made early attempts to establish a foothold in Myanmar, seeking to control key ports for trade purposes. Their influence, however, was limited, and the Dutch soon eclipsed them in prominence. The Dutch managed to establish trading posts and fortifications in key coastal areas, while also engaging in diplomatic exchanges with the Myanmar rulers.

The 18th century saw the rise of the British Empire as a dominant force in the region. The British East India Company, fueled by its expansionist policies, gradually extended its control over parts of India, which had significant implications for Myanmar. The British sought to establish influence and control in Myanmar to safeguard their interests in the Indian subcontinent.

The First Anglo-Burmese War (1824-1826) marked a turning point. The British, with superior naval power and tactics, defeated the Burmese forces, resulting in the signing of the Treaty of Yandabo. This treaty ceded significant territories to the British, including coastal areas and parts of southern Myanmar. The Second Anglo-Burmese War (1852) further eroded Myanmar's sovereignty. The British captured the city of Pegu and expanded their control over lower Myanmar. The British colonial administration introduced various reforms, aiming to modernize administration and facilitate trade, but these changes often clashed with local customs and traditions.

The British gradually consolidated their control over Myanmar, and by the late 19th century, the entire country had fallen under British colonial rule. This marked the end of Myanmar's sovereignty and the beginning of a period of British exploitation of its resources and manpower.

The colonial era was marked by both economic exploitation and cultural transformation. British policies led to economic changes, including the growth of cash crop cultivation and the expansion of infrastructure. However, these changes often came at the expense of local populations and traditional ways of life.

The arrival of the Europeans, with their colonial ambitions and shifting power dynamics, reshaped Myanmar's destiny. The legacy of this era remains complex, with lasting impacts on the country's political, economic, and cultural landscape. Myanmar's struggle for independence, which emerged in the 20th century, was deeply rooted in the experiences of colonial rule and the desire for self-determination in the face of foreign domination.

Burmese Wars and British Annexation

In the tumultuous landscape of Myanmar's history, the 19th century was marked by a series of conflicts and power struggles that ultimately led to British annexation. This chapter delves into the Burmese Wars and the subsequent annexation, shedding light on the intricate web of events that shaped Myanmar's fate.

The First Anglo-Burmese War (1824-1826) set the stage for these conflicts. Triggered by disputes over trade, territory, and British interests in India, the war was characterized by British naval superiority and tactical innovations. The British forces, led by General Archibald Campbell, captured key Burmese territories and forced the Burmese to sign the Treaty of Yandabo.

The treaty, which concluded the First Anglo-Burmese War, had far-reaching consequences. Myanmar ceded territories in Assam, Manipur, and Arakan to the British, significantly altering the geopolitical landscape. The war demonstrated the British East India Company's expansionist agenda and established the precedent for future conflicts.

The Second Anglo-Burmese War (1852) followed in the wake of further territorial disputes and British economic interests. The British forces captured the Burmese city of Pegu, leading to the annexation of lower Myanmar. This marked the beginning of British colonial rule over the region, as Myanmar's sovereignty continued to erode.

The Third Anglo-Burmese War (1885) proved to be the final blow to Myanmar's independence. It was precipitated by tensions over Upper Burma, economic interests, and the British perception of instability in the region. The British accused the Burmese king, Thibaw Min, of mistreatment of British merchants and officially annexed the entire country on January 1, 1886.

The aftermath of the annexation was marked by significant changes. The British colonial administration introduced various reforms aimed at modernizing administration, infrastructure, and economic practices. However, these changes often clashed with local customs and traditions, leading to tensions and resistance.

The annexation also fueled the emergence of a strong nationalist movement in Myanmar. Figures like General Aung San and U Nu would go on to play pivotal roles in the country's quest for independence in the 20th century. The annexation period is remembered as a time of both exploitation and the seeds of Myanmar's fight for self-determination.

The Burmese Wars and the subsequent annexation by the British Empire significantly altered Myanmar's political and cultural trajectory. The country's sovereignty was compromised, and its destiny was now intertwined with British colonial rule. The conflicts of this era remain a critical juncture in Myanmar's history, shaping the nation's resilience and aspirations for the decades to come.

Colonial Impact: Cultural Transformations and Resistance

The colonial era marked a period of profound change and upheaval in Myanmar's history, as the country came under British rule. This chapter explores the multifaceted impact of colonialism, from cultural transformations to the emergence of resistance movements that shaped Myanmar's identity and destiny.

The British colonial administration introduced a range of reforms aimed at modernizing Myanmar's governance and economy. Infrastructure development, including railways and telecommunication networks, altered the physical landscape and connected previously isolated regions. These changes, while contributing to economic growth, often disrupted traditional ways of life.

One of the most significant cultural transformations was the introduction of Western education and values. British-style schools were established, introducing new curricula, languages, and educational philosophies. While this modern education provided opportunities for some, it also created a disconnect between traditional practices and the new values being promoted.

Language became a contentious issue during the colonial era. English was promoted as the language of administration, trade, and education. This shift had profound implications for Myanmar's cultural identity, as traditional languages and scripts were marginalized.

However, it also facilitated communication with the wider world and offered access to global knowledge.

The British colonial administration's policies often clashed with local customs and traditions. Land ownership and taxation systems were restructured, affecting rural communities that depended on traditional agricultural practices. The introduction of a cash economy and new economic structures disrupted existing societal norms.

Resistance to colonial rule emerged through various channels. Nationalist movements began to gain traction, fueled by the desire for self-determination and a renewed sense of cultural identity. Political figures like General Aung San and U Nu spearheaded these movements, advocating for independence and a return to traditional values.

The Saya San Rebellion (1930-1932) stands as an example of armed resistance against British rule. Led by Saya San, a charismatic leader, the rebellion was fueled by grievances over land rights and oppressive colonial policies. The rebellion was suppressed, but it revealed the underlying tensions between the colonial administration and local populations.

World War II brought further disruption as Myanmar became a battleground between the British and Japanese forces. The Japanese occupied Myanmar, promising independence, but their rule was marked by economic exploitation and brutality. The wartime experience further galvanized nationalist sentiments and resistance movements.

The colonial era laid the groundwork for Myanmar's struggle for independence. The emerging political consciousness and cultural revival during this period would culminate in Myanmar's quest for self-determination in the post-war years. The impact of colonialism, while marked by cultural transformations and exploitation, also sowed the seeds of resilience and determination that would shape Myanmar's path toward sovereignty.

Japanese Occupation and World War II

The tumultuous era of World War II left an indelible mark on Myanmar's history, as the country became a theater of conflict and experienced a shift in power dynamics during the Japanese occupation. This chapter delves into the impact of World War II on Myanmar, highlighting the complexities of the Japanese occupation and its repercussions.

The outbreak of World War II in 1939 set off a chain of events that would reshape the global political landscape. Myanmar, then under British colonial rule, found itself drawn into the conflict as the Japanese expanded their reach across Southeast Asia.

In 1942, Japanese forces swiftly advanced through Southeast Asia, including Myanmar. The British, facing challenges on multiple fronts, were unable to prevent the Japanese occupation. The Japanese promised Myanmar independence from British colonial rule, tapping into the nationalist sentiments that had been brewing for decades.

The Japanese occupation was a complex period marked by both collaboration and resistance. The promise of independence attracted some local leaders who saw an opportunity to cooperate with the Japanese. However, this collaboration often came at a high cost, as the Japanese exploited Myanmar's resources and subjected the population to economic hardship.

Myanmar's experience under Japanese rule varied by region. While some areas faced economic hardships due to

Japanese policies, others experienced brutal repression and forced labor. The imposition of Japanese culture and language further fueled tensions, as it clashed with Myanmar's cultural identity.

The period also witnessed the emergence of resistance movements against both Japanese and British rule. The Anti-Fascist People's Freedom League (AFPFL), led by figures like General Aung San, collaborated with the Allies in their efforts against the Axis powers. These movements laid the foundation for post-war political developments.

As World War II drew to a close, Allied forces launched counteroffensives across Southeast Asia. In 1945, British forces re-entered Myanmar, gradually liberating the country from Japanese occupation. The challenges of wartime occupation had left Myanmar scarred, with economic devastation and social disruptions.

The end of World War II marked a turning point in Myanmar's history. The return of British colonial forces was met with a renewed desire for self-determination and independence. The wartime experience, marked by collaboration, resistance, and the complexities of foreign occupation, laid the groundwork for Myanmar's post-war struggles and its journey toward sovereignty.

Burma Road to Independence: Post-war Struggles and Aung San

As the echoes of World War II subsided, Myanmar embarked on a new chapter in its history—a journey towards independence. This chapter unravels the post-war struggles, the emergence of key figures like General Aung San, and the intricate dynamics that shaped Myanmar's path to sovereignty.

The end of World War II brought both relief and uncertainty to Myanmar. While the Allied victory marked the liberation from Japanese occupation, it also posed challenges in rebuilding the nation. The economic devastation left behind by the war exacerbated social and political tensions.

The wartime experience had a profound impact on Myanmar's political consciousness. The Anti-Fascist People's Freedom League (AFPFL), led by figures like General Aung San, emerged as a unifying force among the diverse ethnic groups of Myanmar. The AFPFL sought to address the aspirations of the people for self-determination and independence.

Aung San, a charismatic and visionary leader, played a pivotal role in Myanmar's post-war struggle for independence. His collaboration with the Allies during the war solidified his standing among the Myanmar people. Aung San's pragmatism, strategic thinking, and ability to bridge ethnic divides made him a beacon of hope in the tumultuous post-war landscape.

Negotiations with the British administration were central to Myanmar's pursuit of independence. The Panglong Agreement of 1947, a landmark moment in Myanmar's history, symbolized a united front among various ethnic groups. The agreement laid the foundation for a future federal state that respected the rights and identities of all ethnicities.

Tragedy struck in 1947 when Aung San and several of his colleagues were assassinated. Despite his untimely death, Aung San's legacy endured. His vision for an inclusive and independent Myanmar continued to inspire the nation's leaders and citizens in the challenging years that followed.

The years leading up to independence were marked by political maneuvering and negotiations. The talks with the British led to the establishment of the transitional government and the eventual transfer of power. On January 4, 1948, Myanmar officially gained independence, marking the end of colonial rule and the dawn of a new era.

However, the journey towards stability was fraught with challenges. Ethnic conflicts, economic disparities, and political divisions tested the newly formed nation. The spirit of unity that had characterized the struggle for independence was put to the test as Myanmar grappled with the complexities of nation-building.

Union of Burma: Early Years of Sovereignty and Challenges

With the dawn of independence on January 4, 1948, Myanmar embarked on a new phase of its history—the era of the Union of Burma. This chapter delves into the early years of Myanmar's sovereignty, the complexities of nation-building, and the challenges that accompanied its newfound independence.

The Union of Burma's formation was marked by a spirit of optimism and the collective desire to forge a united nation. As the nation's leaders grappled with the task of governing a diverse population, they faced the monumental challenge of reconciling ethnic identities and aspirations within the framework of a single nation.

Ethnic diversity became a defining feature of the Union of Burma's early years. The Panglong Agreement of 1947, which emphasized federalism and the recognition of ethnic rights, served as a foundational document for the new nation. However, implementing this vision proved to be a complex endeavor, as ethnic tensions and grievances resurfaced over time.

The challenges of nation-building extended beyond ethnic issues. Economic disparities, infrastructure deficits, and limited resources presented hurdles for the young nation's development. The legacy of colonial rule, with its exploitative economic structures and educational disparities, added layers of complexity to the task of building a self-sufficient and equitable society.

The political landscape of the Union of Burma was marked by competing ideologies and visions for the nation's future. The period saw the rise of different political parties, each with its own agenda and approach to governance. This political diversity reflected the complexities of a society in transition, striving to define its identity and direction.

The nascent democracy faced internal and external challenges. The Karen National Union (KNU) and other ethnic armed groups sought greater autonomy, leading to armed conflicts that threatened stability. Myanmar's position in the global arena was also shaped by the Cold War dynamics, as the nation navigated between various political alignments.

Economic development was a pressing concern. Efforts were made to modernize agriculture, industry, and infrastructure, but progress was often hindered by financial constraints and political uncertainties. Myanmar's economic trajectory was further influenced by global factors, including shifts in international trade and aid relationships.

The early years of the Union of Burma saw strides in education and cultural revival. Steps were taken to promote indigenous languages, literature, and art, as the nation sought to preserve its cultural heritage in the face of modernization. However, the task of balancing traditional values with the demands of progress remained a challenge.

The challenges faced by the Union of Burma's early years underscored the complexities of nation-building and the need for inclusive governance. The nation's leaders were tasked with fostering unity amidst diversity, addressing economic disparities, and defining Myanmar's role in the global community. As the Union of Burma navigated its formative years, its successes and struggles laid the groundwork for the nation's ongoing evolution, reflecting the resilience and aspirations of its people.

1950s Political Turmoil and Ethnic Diversity

The 1950s marked a turbulent period in Myanmar's history, as the newly independent nation grappled with political challenges, ideological shifts, and the complexities of its diverse ethnic landscape. This chapter delves into the political dynamics and ethnic diversity that characterized this era of change.

The early years of the decade were characterized by shifting political alignments and ideological debates. The Anti-Fascist People's Freedom League (AFPFL), once a unifying force, began to fracture along ideological lines. The split between the factions led by U Nu and Ba Swe highlighted differing visions for Myanmar's future.

Ethnic diversity remained a prominent theme in Myanmar's political landscape. The Panglong Agreement of 1947, which aimed to recognize the rights and autonomy of ethnic groups, faced difficulties in implementation. Ethnic tensions flared, and demands for greater autonomy from groups like the Karen National Union (KNU) and others led to armed conflicts.

The Karen insurgency, fueled by grievances over autonomy and cultural preservation, became a central challenge to the government's authority. The KNU's armed struggle sought to secure political and cultural rights for the Karen people, further highlighting the complex task of reconciling diverse ethnic identities within a unified nation.

The decade witnessed several political transitions. In 1958, U Nu's government gave way to a caretaker administration led by Ne Win. The political landscape remained volatile, with successive governments struggling to balance the demands of ethnic groups, ideological factions, and economic development.

The 1950s also saw the rise of communism as a political force. The Communist Party of Burma (CPB), drawing inspiration from Marxist-Leninist ideologies, gained traction in rural areas. Their armed insurgency challenged the government's control, leading to conflict that deepened political instability.

Economic challenges further exacerbated the political turmoil. Myanmar's attempts at economic development were hindered by inadequate infrastructure, limited resources, and global economic fluctuations. These challenges fueled frustrations among the population, contributing to the volatile political climate.

Myanmar's foreign relations were influenced by the Cold War context. The nation navigated between various alignments, seeking aid and support from different sources. The geopolitical pressures added another layer of complexity to the internal challenges Myanmar faced.

The 1950s concluded with a coup in 1962, led by General Ne Win. This marked a turning point as the nation transitioned to military rule, a period that would significantly impact Myanmar's trajectory in the following decades. The political turmoil of the 1950s highlighted the intricacies of governance in a diverse nation and underscored the importance of addressing ethnic aspirations, economic development, and political stability.

Ne Win's Era: Military Rule and Isolationism

The onset of military rule under General Ne Win marked a pivotal chapter in Myanmar's history, shaping the nation's trajectory for decades to come. This chapter delves into the Ne Win era, characterized by authoritarian governance, isolationism, and the enduring impact of military rule.

Ne Win's coup in 1962 toppled the civilian government, initiating a period of military rule that would span nearly three decades. His regime was characterized by a centralized and autocratic style of governance, which aimed to assert control over all aspects of Myanmar's society and economy.

One of the defining features of Ne Win's era was his implementation of the Burmese Way to Socialism. This policy, which aimed to establish a self-reliant socialist state, led to the nationalization of industries and the suppression of private enterprise. However, this approach resulted in economic stagnation and decline, leading to widespread poverty and the collapse of Myanmar's once-thriving economy.

Ne Win's regime also enforced strict censorship and control over the media, limiting the flow of information and stifling dissent. Political opposition was systematically suppressed, and any perceived threats to the regime were met with harsh crackdowns. This atmosphere of repression created a climate of fear and silence throughout the nation.

Isolationism became a hallmark of Ne Win's rule. His government pursued a policy of self-reliance and non-alignment with foreign powers, resulting in Myanmar's detachment from the global community. This isolation had severe consequences for the nation's development, as it limited access to international trade, aid, and investment.

Ethnic tensions continued to simmer during Ne Win's era. Armed conflicts with various ethnic groups persisted, fueled by grievances over autonomy and cultural rights. The government's attempts to forcibly assimilate ethnic minorities and suppress their cultural identities further exacerbated these tensions. The economic mismanagement and political repression of the Ne Win era culminated in the 1988 uprising. Mass protests against the regime's policies and human rights abuses erupted across the country, demanding democratic reforms and an end to military rule. The government's violent crackdown on the protests led to a tragic loss of life and solidified the regime's reputation for brutality.

The turmoil of 1988 forced Ne Win to resign, but it did not mark the end of military rule. The State Law and Order Restoration Council (SLORC), led by General Saw Maung, took power and continued the repressive policies of the previous regime.

Ne Win's era left a profound and lasting impact on Myanmar. The policies of isolationism, economic mismanagement, and political repression hindered the nation's development and perpetuated a cycle of poverty and human rights abuses. The era underscored the need for political reform, democracy, and a more inclusive approach to governance—an imperative that would shape Myanmar's future struggles and aspirations.

1988 Uprising and Pro-Democracy Movements

The year 1988 stands as a watershed moment in Myanmar's history, as the nation witnessed a groundswell of pro-democracy movements and a powerful uprising that shook the foundations of the authoritarian regime. This chapter delves into the events of the 1988 uprising and the emergence of pro-democracy movements that would shape Myanmar's trajectory.

The backdrop to the 1988 uprising was decades of authoritarian rule under the military regime led by General Ne Win. Economic mismanagement, political repression, and human rights abuses had fueled widespread discontent among the population, creating a powder keg of frustration and grievances.

The catalyst for the uprising was a sharp increase in the prices of essential goods and services, triggering protests across the nation. What began as student-led demonstrations soon escalated into a massive movement demanding democratic reforms, an end to military rule, and respect for human rights. The protests gained momentum and spread to various parts of the country.

The government's response to the protests was brutal. The military regime deployed security forces to suppress the demonstrations, resulting in violent clashes and loss of life. The government's heavy-handed tactics only fueled the anger of the protesters, and the situation quickly spiraled into a full-blown uprising.

The 1988 uprising saw people from all walks of life coming together in an unprecedented show of unity. Students, workers, monks, and civilians of all ages joined hands to demand change and democracy. The movement transcended ethnic and religious lines, reflecting the shared desire for a brighter future for Myanmar.

The uprising also saw the emergence of key figures who would go on to play pivotal roles in Myanmar's pro-democracy movement. Aung San Suu Kyi, daughter of General Aung San, became a prominent symbol of resistance. Her calls for nonviolent protest and democratic principles resonated deeply with the people.

As the uprising intensified, the government declared martial law and eventually implemented a military coup in September 1988. The State Law and Order Restoration Council (SLORC), led by General Saw Maung, took power and initiated a brutal crackdown on dissent. The regime's violent response to the protests resulted in a tragic loss of life and led to further international isolation.

Despite the suppression, the 1988 uprising marked a turning point. The pro-democracy movements had ignited a flame of hope for change that could not be extinguished. The events of 1988 laid the groundwork for future struggles for democracy and human rights, setting the stage for Myanmar's ongoing journey towards a more inclusive and democratic society. The legacy of the 1988 uprising remains a reminder of the resilience and courage of the Myanmar people in the face of adversity.

Nobel Laureate Aung San Suu Kyi's Influence

The influence of Nobel laureate Aung San Suu Kyi on Myanmar's history is profound and far-reaching. Her unwavering commitment to democracy, human rights, and nonviolent resistance has earned her a place as a prominent global figure and a symbol of hope for Myanmar's future. This chapter delves into Aung San Suu Kyi's influence, her role in shaping Myanmar's political landscape, and the complexities of her legacy.

Aung San Suu Kyi was born in 1945, the daughter of Myanmar's independence hero, General Aung San. Her upbringing was marked by political awareness and a strong sense of duty to her country. After studying abroad and raising a family, she returned to Myanmar in 1988, just as the country was being swept by pro-democracy movements.

Her emergence as a pro-democracy leader was swift. Her speeches advocating for democracy and human rights resonated deeply with the Myanmar people, earning her a place as a unifying figure in the midst of political turmoil. Her call for nonviolent resistance and her willingness to stand up against the military regime captured the nation's imagination.

In 1990, the National League for Democracy (NLD), led by Aung San Suu Kyi, won a landslide victory in the general elections. However, the military junta refused to honor the results, plunging the nation into further uncertainty. Aung

San Suu Kyi's perseverance in the face of adversity and her unwavering commitment to democratic ideals solidified her status as a symbol of resistance.

Her influence extended beyond Myanmar's borders. In 1991, Aung San Suu Kyi was awarded the Nobel Peace Prize for her nonviolent struggle for democracy and human rights. The international recognition bolstered her global stature and drew attention to the plight of Myanmar under military rule.

Throughout the years, Aung San Suu Kyi's influence remained a beacon of hope for the Myanmar people. Her resilience in the face of house arrest, personal sacrifice, and the regime's attempts to silence her spoke volumes about her dedication to her country's freedom.

Her eventual release from house arrest in 2010 marked a turning point. The political landscape of Myanmar was evolving, and Aung San Suu Kyi stepped onto the world stage once again, this time as a politician. The 2015 general elections saw the NLD secure a resounding victory, and Aung San Suu Kyi assumed the role of State Counsellor, a de facto leader.

However, her leadership was not without controversy. As Myanmar transitioned to a civilian government, challenges remained—ethnic conflicts, human rights violations, and the complex balance between military and civilian authority. Aung San Suu Kyi's handling of issues such as the Rohingya crisis drew criticism and raised questions about her commitment to human rights.

Myanmar's Ethnic Conflicts: Paths to Reconciliation

Myanmar's history has been marked by ethnic diversity and the complexities that come with it. The nation's patchwork of ethnic groups, each with their own identities, languages, and histories, has at times been a source of strength and at other times a catalyst for conflict. This chapter delves into the ethnic conflicts that have shaped Myanmar's past and explores the various paths towards reconciliation.

Ethnic tensions in Myanmar have deep historical roots. The diversity of ethnic groups, including the Bamar, Shan, Karen, Kachin, and others, has often led to struggles over resources, territory, and cultural identity. These tensions were exacerbated by colonial policies that often pitted different ethnic groups against each other.

After gaining independence, Myanmar faced the daunting task of unifying its diverse population under a single national identity. The Panglong Agreement of 1947 was an early attempt at addressing ethnic aspirations, but its implementation faced challenges. The subsequent decades saw sporadic armed conflicts between ethnic groups and the central government.

The complexity of Myanmar's ethnic conflicts was further intensified by the military's grip on power. The centralization of authority and suppression of ethnic identities under military regimes often exacerbated existing tensions. As ethnic groups sought greater autonomy and recognition, the government responded with military force.

The Karen National Union (KNU), the Kachin Independence Organization (KIO), and other ethnic armed groups engaged in armed struggles to secure their rights and autonomy. These conflicts resulted in displacement, human rights abuses, and a cycle of violence that deeply affected the lives of the people in conflict-affected areas.

Efforts at reconciliation and peace have been ongoing for years. The 2015 Nationwide Ceasefire Agreement (NCA) was a significant milestone, signed between the government and several ethnic armed groups. While the NCA represented progress, not all groups were on board, and the path to a comprehensive peace remained elusive.

The peace process faced challenges due to its complexity and the differing interests of various stakeholders. The underlying issues of land rights, resource sharing, political representation, and cultural recognition remained contentious. Balancing these demands within the framework of a unified nation was a daunting task.

Reconciliation efforts also faced obstacles in the form of deep-seated mistrust, historical grievances, and the legacy of violence. Overcoming these hurdles required a multifaceted approach that involved not only political negotiations but also efforts to heal wounds, rebuild communities, and foster understanding between different ethnic groups.

The 2020 elections were seen as a step forward in Myanmar's democratization, and there were hopes that the civilian government would continue to prioritize ethnic reconciliation. However, the military coup in February 2021 has raised new challenges, casting uncertainty on the prospects for peaceful coexistence and resolution of ethnic conflicts.

The paths to reconciliation in Myanmar are complex and multifaceted. They require addressing historical grievances, recognizing the rights and identities of ethnic groups, and fostering a sense of inclusivity within the nation. Achieving lasting peace will demand a combination of political negotiations, grassroots efforts, and a genuine commitment to understanding and respecting the diverse tapestry of Myanmar's people.

Emergence of Naypyidaw: New Capital and Political Shifts

The emergence of Naypyidaw as Myanmar's new capital marked a significant chapter in the nation's history, with far-reaching implications for its political landscape and governance. This chapter delves into the circumstances leading to the creation of Naypyidaw, the rationale behind its establishment, and the subsequent shifts in Myanmar's political dynamics.

The idea of relocating the capital had been discussed for decades before it materialized. Yangon (formerly Rangoon), with its historical significance and economic prominence, had long been the capital of Myanmar. However, concerns about its vulnerability to natural disasters and congestion led to discussions about moving the capital to a more secure and planned location.

In 2005, the Myanmar government announced its decision to establish a new capital, Naypyidaw, located about 200 miles north of Yangon. The decision to build a new capital from scratch was ambitious and unprecedented, requiring extensive infrastructure development and urban planning.

The choice of Naypyidaw as the new capital was not without controversy. The secrecy surrounding the decision-making process, combined with the magnitude of the project, raised questions about the government's motives. Some speculated that the move was driven by security concerns, while others saw it as a way to consolidate the military regime's grip on power.

The construction of Naypyidaw was shrouded in secrecy, with limited information available to the public. The city's development was expedited, and government offices, residential areas, and infrastructure were built in a remarkably short period. The government's ability to undertake such a massive endeavor highlighted its authority and control over resources.

Naypyidaw's emergence brought about a shift in Myanmar's political dynamics. The city was designed to be a sprawling administrative and political hub, hosting government ministries, military headquarters, and foreign embassies. The move symbolized a departure from Yangon's historical and economic centrality, reflecting the military regime's focus on consolidating its power and isolating itself from external influences.

The political transition in Myanmar in the early 2010s marked a new phase in Naypyidaw's role. The military junta began to make limited reforms, including the release of Aung San Suu Kyi from house arrest and the gradual opening of the country to the international community. Naypyidaw became a platform for diplomatic engagement, as Myanmar sought to mend its international relations.

Naypyidaw's creation also reflected the broader challenges of Myanmar's political landscape. The city's isolation and lack of organic growth raised questions about its sustainability and whether it truly represented the aspirations of the Myanmar people. The absence of a historical or cultural connection with the capital posed challenges in fostering a sense of national identity.

Rohingya Crisis and International Scrutiny

The Rohingya crisis is a tragic chapter in Myanmar's history that has captured global attention and raised pressing questions about human rights, identity, and the responsibilities of the international community. This chapter delves into the origins of the Rohingya crisis, the events that unfolded, and the international response that followed.

The Rohingya are an ethnic minority group predominantly residing in Rakhine State, western Myanmar. Their history in the region dates back centuries, but their identity and citizenship have been disputed by the Myanmar government. The tensions between the Rohingya and the government escalated over time, with discriminatory policies and violence exacerbating their vulnerability.

The crisis reached a critical point in August 2017 when violence erupted in Rakhine State. The Myanmar military, responding to attacks by Rohingya insurgents, launched a brutal crackdown on Rohingya communities. Reports emerged of widespread atrocities, including killings, sexual violence, and the burning of villages. This triggered a massive exodus, with hundreds of thousands of Rohingya fleeing across the border to Bangladesh.

The international community was swift to condemn the violence and human rights abuses. The United Nations and various human rights organizations documented the atrocities, and the situation attracted global attention. The term "ethnic cleansing" was widely used to describe the actions of the Myanmar military against the Rohingya population.

The crisis also put Aung San Suu Kyi, Myanmar's de facto leader, under scrutiny. Her response to the crisis garnered criticism for what many perceived as inadequate acknowledgment of the severity of the situation and the government's role. The situation highlighted the challenges of balancing political priorities and human rights obligations.

The Rohingya crisis had far-reaching consequences for regional stability. The influx of Rohingya refugees into Bangladesh placed immense strain on the country's resources and infrastructure. The crisis also strained relations between Myanmar and its neighbors, particularly Bangladesh.

International efforts to address the crisis included calls for accountability and justice. The International Criminal Court (ICC) initiated investigations into alleged crimes against humanity committed against the Rohingya. Various human rights bodies and international organizations demanded that Myanmar take responsibility for its actions and ensure the safe return of the Rohingya refugees.

The Rohingya crisis raised complex questions about identity, citizenship, and the rights of minority groups. The Myanmar government denied citizenship to the Rohingya, rendering them stateless and vulnerable. This crisis shed light on the broader issue of ethnic tensions within Myanmar and the urgent need for addressing the plight of minority groups.

The international response was a mix of condemnation, diplomatic pressure, and aid efforts. Sanctions were imposed on some Myanmar military officials, and humanitarian organizations worked to provide assistance to Rohingya refugees. However, finding a comprehensive solution that addresses the root causes of the crisis, ensures justice for the victims, and guarantees the rights of the Rohingya remains an ongoing challenge.

The Rohingya crisis and the international scrutiny it brought to Myanmar underscore the complexities of addressing human rights abuses, minority rights, and the responsibilities of the international community. The crisis serves as a reminder of the urgent need for reconciliation, accountability, and efforts to prevent such tragedies from occurring in the future.

Economic Reforms: Opening Up to the Global Market

Myanmar's history has been marked by economic challenges stemming from colonial rule, isolationist policies, and mismanagement. However, in recent years, the nation has embarked on a path of economic reforms aimed at integrating into the global market and fostering sustainable development. This chapter delves into the economic reforms, policy shifts, and their impact on Myanmar's economic landscape.

Myanmar's economic landscape prior to the reforms was characterized by state control, limited foreign investment, and isolation from the global economy. Decades of military rule had resulted in an economy that was largely closed off from international trade and investment, leading to stagnation and poverty.

The turning point came in 2011, when the government initiated a series of economic reforms aimed at opening up the country to the global market. These reforms included liberalizing trade, simplifying regulations, and encouraging foreign investment. The government's goal was to attract much-needed capital, technology, and expertise to revitalize the economy.

One of the most significant reforms was the introduction of the Foreign Investment Law in 2012. This law aimed to provide incentives for foreign investors, including tax breaks and guarantees of property rights. The government also established special economic zones to attract investment and foster industrial growth.

The reforms led to a surge in foreign investment and a diversification of the economy. Sectors such as telecommunications, energy, and manufacturing attracted significant foreign capital, resulting in new job opportunities and increased economic activity. The opening up of the banking sector also facilitated access to financial services and capital.

Myanmar's participation in the ASEAN Economic Community (AEC) further facilitated economic integration. The nation's strategic location and natural resources positioned it as a potential hub for trade and investment in Southeast Asia. The government's commitment to regional cooperation and trade agreements signaled its willingness to engage with neighboring countries.

Despite these positive developments, challenges remained. Myanmar's infrastructure deficit and bureaucratic hurdles presented obstacles to investment and growth. Income inequality, inadequate education and healthcare, and the need for improved governance continued to be areas of concern. The country also faced the delicate task of balancing economic growth with social and environmental sustainability.

The reforms had a significant impact on Myanmar's international image. The nation's reintegration into the global economy was met with cautious optimism from the international community. Trade agreements and economic partnerships were established with countries such as China, India, and Japan, while multinational corporations began exploring business opportunities in Myanmar.

However, the rapid pace of change also brought its own set of challenges. The influx of foreign investment raised concerns about land rights, environmental sustainability, and equitable wealth distribution. The government's ability to manage these complexities while ensuring benefits for the wider population was put to the test.

The economic reforms, while promising, also highlighted the need for comprehensive development strategies that address poverty reduction, infrastructure development, and social welfare. The challenge of sustaining economic growth while maintaining social stability and environmental integrity remains an ongoing endeavor for Myanmar.

The opening up of Myanmar's economy to the global market marked a significant departure from decades of isolation. The reforms signaled the nation's aspirations for development, integration, and engagement with the international community. As Myanmar continues on its economic journey, the balance between attracting foreign investment, promoting inclusive growth, and addressing social challenges will shape the nation's path towards a more prosperous and sustainable future.

Cultural Heritage and Artistic Traditions

Myanmar's rich cultural heritage and artistic traditions have evolved over centuries, shaped by diverse ethnic influences, religious beliefs, and historical events. This chapter delves into the multifaceted tapestry of Myanmar's cultural identity, exploring its artistic expressions, traditional practices, and the challenges of preserving this heritage in a changing world.

Cultural heritage in Myanmar is a reflection of the nation's vibrant ethnic diversity. With over 135 distinct ethnic groups, each with its own language, customs, and artistic practices, Myanmar boasts a kaleidoscope of traditions that contribute to its unique identity. The Bamar, the majority ethnic group, have historically played a central role in shaping the nation's culture.

Religion has been a pivotal factor in shaping Myanmar's cultural landscape. Theravada Buddhism has had a profound influence on the artistic and cultural expressions of the country. Monasteries, pagodas, and temples dot the landscape, showcasing intricate architectural designs, decorative art, and religious sculptures.

Buddhist art in Myanmar is characterized by its distinctive style, often incorporating symbolic motifs and intricate detailing. The Shwedagon Pagoda in Yangon, a revered site, is a prime example of Myanmar's rich artistic heritage. Its golden spire, adorned with jewels and engravings, reflects the devotion and craftsmanship of generations.

Traditional performing arts hold a special place in Myanmar's culture. Dance, music, and theater play an essential role in religious ceremonies, festivals, and storytelling. Traditional dance forms like the graceful "pwe" and the puppetry art of "yoke thé" continue to captivate audiences with their elegance and cultural significance.

Myanmar's literary tradition has a long history, with its roots in ancient epics, folk tales, and Buddhist scriptures. The "Jataka" stories, depicting the previous lives of the Buddha, are a prominent example of Myanmar's literary heritage. Modern literature has also evolved, reflecting the nation's changing social and political landscape.

The challenges of preserving Myanmar's cultural heritage are manifold. Urbanization, modernization, and globalization have brought about changes that threaten traditional practices and architectural treasures. Rapid development often comes at the expense of historical sites and cultural authenticity.

The shift towards a more open society also presents both opportunities and challenges for cultural preservation. While increased international engagement can help promote Myanmar's cultural heritage on a global stage, it also raises concerns about cultural appropriation and the preservation of traditional knowledge.

Efforts to safeguard Myanmar's cultural heritage have included initiatives to restore and conserve historical sites, promote traditional arts, and document indigenous knowledge. National and international organizations have collaborated to protect and promote cultural practices, and museums play a crucial role in preserving and showcasing Myanmar's artistic legacy.

The arts have also played a role in shaping the nation's social and political narratives. Creative expressions, such as literature and visual arts, have served as platforms for both dissent and celebration. Artists have used their craft to reflect on Myanmar's history, identity, and aspirations.

Myanmar's Natural Wonders: Flora, Fauna, and Biodiversity

Myanmar's breathtaking landscapes are home to a diverse array of flora, fauna, and ecosystems, making it a biodiversity hotspot of global significance. This chapter explores the natural wonders that adorn Myanmar's terrain, the unique species that inhabit its forests and waters, and the challenges of conserving this rich biodiversity in the face of modernization.

The country's geographical diversity, stretching from the Himalayas in the north to the Andaman Sea in the south, contributes to its remarkable biodiversity. Lush rainforests, sprawling plains, mist-covered mountains, and pristine coastlines create a variety of habitats that support an astounding array of plant and animal life.

Myanmar's forests are rich with flora, including a multitude of tree species, orchids, and medicinal plants. The Hukaung Valley Wildlife Sanctuary is home to a vast expanse of untouched forests, housing species like the elusive snow leopard and the rare red panda. The nation's forests also hold cultural significance, serving as sites for religious practices and traditional knowledge.

The Irrawaddy River, the lifeline of Myanmar, sustains a variety of aquatic life. The Irrawaddy dolphin, a freshwater species, inhabits the river's waters. Coastal areas, such as the Myeik Archipelago, are home to coral reefs, sea turtles, and diverse marine life. These marine ecosystems contribute to the nation's unique ecological tapestry.

Myanmar's avian diversity is equally remarkable, with over a thousand bird species documented. The Hlawga National Park, near Yangon, is a prime birdwatching destination. Migratory birds, such as the rare spoon-billed sandpiper, also rely on Myanmar's wetlands as stopovers on their journeys.

The nation's fauna also includes iconic species like the Asian elephant and the Burmese python. The country's forests provide habitats for various primates, including gibbons and macaques. Endangered species like the tiger and the pangolin face threats due to habitat loss and illegal wildlife trade.

The biodiversity of Myanmar also holds valuable potential for scientific discovery. The nation's forests are a treasure trove of plant species with medicinal and ecological significance. The exploration of its ecosystems can offer insights into the interconnections between biodiversity, climate, and human well-being.

Conservation efforts in Myanmar face a delicate balance between development and safeguarding biodiversity. Deforestation, habitat degradation, and wildlife trafficking remain pressing challenges. The expansion of agricultural land, infrastructure projects, and the impacts of climate change all pose risks to the nation's natural heritage.

National parks and protected areas play a crucial role in preserving Myanmar's biodiversity. Institutions like the Wildlife Conservation Society and local NGOs collaborate to raise awareness, enforce regulations, and promote sustainable practices. Initiatives to combat illegal wildlife trade and promote community-based conservation have gained traction.

The government's commitment to conservation is evident through policies and international agreements. Myanmar is a signatory to the Convention on Biological Diversity and has designated several areas as UNESCO Biosphere Reserves. The nation's participation in initiatives like the Global Tiger Recovery Program reflects its dedication to safeguarding endangered species.

Gastronomic Journey: Exploring Myanmar's Cuisine

Myanmar's cuisine is a reflection of its rich cultural heritage, influenced by its diverse ethnic groups, historical trade routes, and agricultural bounty. This chapter embarks on a gastronomic journey through the flavors, ingredients, and culinary traditions that define Myanmar's unique cuisine, offering a glimpse into the nation's culinary tapestry.

Rice is the staple of Myanmar's cuisine, with nearly every meal accompanied by a bowl of steamed rice. The term "htamin" refers to cooked rice, and it's an essential component of the Myanmar diet. Rice is often served with a variety of curries, vegetables, and condiments.

Curries play a central role in Myanmar's culinary landscape. Mohinga, considered the national dish, is a flavorful fish soup made with rice vermicelli and an array of aromatic herbs and spices. Curries are typically rich in flavor, often combining ingredients like fish, chicken, pork, or beef with a blend of spices, garlic, and onions.

Burmese curries are characterized by the use of "ngapi," a fermented fish or shrimp paste, which adds depth and complexity to the flavors. Another staple condiment is "ngayote," a mixture of dried shrimp, chili, and other seasonings used to add a spicy kick to dishes.

Tea is another integral aspect of Myanmar's culinary culture. Unlike other Southeast Asian countries, tea is consumed as a main course rather than a beverage. Lahpet thoke, or tea leaf salad, is a popular dish that features fermented tea leaves mixed with a medley of ingredients like fried garlic, peanuts, sesame seeds, and dried shrimp.

Street food is a vibrant part of Myanmar's culinary scene. Vendors offer an array of delectable treats, from samosas to skewered meats to fried noodles. The bustling street food markets offer a sensory delight, showcasing the diversity of flavors that Myanmar has to offer.

Myanmar's sweets and desserts reflect its affinity for unique ingredients and flavors. "Mont lone yay paw," a glutinous rice cake wrapped in banana leaves and stuffed with jaggery (palm sugar) and coconut, is a beloved treat. "Shwe yin aye," a cold dessert made with coconut milk, agar jelly, and a medley of colorful ingredients, is often enjoyed on hot days.

Fruits hold a special place in Myanmar's cuisine, with tropical offerings like mangoes, durians, and mangosteens featuring prominently. These fruits are often enjoyed as snacks or desserts, and their vibrant flavors contribute to the nation's culinary diversity.

Myanmar's culinary traditions are deeply intertwined with its social and cultural practices. Sharing a meal with family and friends is an essential part of daily life, often symbolizing camaraderie and hospitality. Special occasions and festivals are marked by elaborate feasts that showcase the diversity of dishes and flavors.

In recent years, Myanmar's cuisine has gained international recognition, drawing interest from food enthusiasts and travelers alike. The nation's culinary heritage is celebrated through culinary festivals, cooking classes, and food tours that offer a window into its traditional and modern interpretations.

Myanmar's gastronomic journey reflects the nation's resilience, creativity, and rich cultural mosaic. As the nation continues to evolve, its cuisine remains a vital thread connecting the past with the present and serving as a dynamic canvas for the flavors, stories, and traditions of Myanmar's people.

Golden Rock and Other Sacred Sites

Myanmar's spiritual and religious fabric is woven with a tapestry of sacred sites that hold deep significance for its people. This chapter takes you on a journey to some of the most revered places of worship, including the iconic Golden Rock, that reflect the nation's devotion, cultural heritage, and spiritual beliefs.

The Golden Rock, or Kyaiktiyo Pagoda, is an awe-inspiring site perched atop a precariously balanced boulder, seemingly defying gravity. Located in the Mon State, this golden-clad pagoda is considered one of the most sacred pilgrimage destinations in Myanmar. Devotees from all walks of life come to pay their respects, making the arduous journey up the mountain to witness this remarkable sight.

Legend has it that the Golden Rock is balanced on a single strand of Buddha's hair, making it a symbol of faith and devotion. Pilgrims often affix gold leaf to the rock as a gesture of merit-making and to seek blessings. The annual Kyaiktiyo Pagoda Festival draws thousands of devotees, creating a vibrant and spiritually charged atmosphere.

The Shwedagon Pagoda, located in Yangon, is another iconic sacred site that stands as a beacon of Myanmar's religious heritage. This gilded stupa is said to enshrine strands of Buddha's hair, making it one of the most revered Buddhist sites in the world. Its towering spire and ornate architecture make it a testament to Myanmar's devotion and architectural prowess.

Buddhism is deeply ingrained in Myanmar's cultural and spiritual identity, and its temples and monasteries are scattered throughout the nation's landscape. The Mahamuni Pagoda in Mandalay is famous for its gilded statue of Buddha, which is coated with layers of gold leaf by devotees. The Sule Pagoda in Yangon serves as a bustling hub of spiritual activity in the heart of the city.

The Shwesandaw Pagoda in Bagan offers panoramic views of the ancient city's stupas and temples, making it a popular spot for sunrise and sunset worship. The Ananda Temple, known as the "Westminster Abbey of Burma," showcases architectural grandeur and historical significance, drawing pilgrims and tourists alike.

Myanmar's religious landscape also includes diverse sites of worship for different faiths. The Koe Thaung Temple in Mrauk U is one of the largest surviving temples in the Arakan region, adorned with intricate carvings that depict scenes from Buddhist scriptures. The Holy Trinity Cathedral in Yangon is a symbol of Myanmar's Christian community, showcasing stunning Gothic architecture.

Sacred sites are not only places of worship but also hubs of cultural exchange and community. They provide a platform for spiritual reflection, cultural expression, and social cohesion. The devotion and rituals practiced at these sites serve as a bridge between the past and the present, connecting generations through shared faith and tradition.

As Myanmar continues to evolve, its sacred sites remain timeless witnesses to the nation's spiritual journey. The interplay between faith, architecture, and cultural heritage is a testament to the enduring significance of these sites. Whether it's the mystical allure of the Golden Rock or the tranquility of a monastery's courtyard, these sacred places embody the soul of Myanmar and offer a window into its profound spirituality.

Bagan Revisited: Preservation Efforts and Modern Challenges

Bagan, with its vast expanse of ancient temples and stupas, stands as a testament to Myanmar's rich historical and cultural heritage. This chapter delves into the ongoing efforts to preserve and protect this archaeological marvel, while also exploring the modern challenges that Bagan faces as it seeks to balance its historical significance with the demands of modernization.

Bagan's archaeological wonders date back to the 9th to 13th centuries, when the Bagan Kingdom flourished as a center of Theravada Buddhism. The region boasts thousands of temples, pagodas, and stupas, creating a breathtaking landscape that draws travelers, historians, and spiritual seekers alike.

Preserving Bagan's heritage has been an ongoing endeavor. In recent years, the Myanmar government, along with international organizations and heritage experts, has worked to conserve and safeguard these ancient structures. The Bagan Archaeological Zone was designated a UNESCO World Heritage Site in 2019, recognizing its global significance and promoting conservation efforts.

One of the challenges in preserving Bagan lies in striking a balance between restoration and authenticity. Some temples have undergone extensive renovation to restore their original grandeur, while others have been left in their original state to showcase the passage of time. The delicate task of restoration involves combining historical accuracy with modern techniques and materials.

Another challenge is managing the impact of tourism on the site. The increasing number of visitors poses risks to the fragile structures and their surroundings. Measures to control foot traffic and protect sensitive areas have been implemented, but finding a balance between accessibility and conservation remains a complex task.

Modern development also presents challenges to Bagan's preservation. The construction of new hotels, roads, and infrastructure can potentially impact the integrity of the site. Striking a harmonious balance between modern amenities and historical preservation is crucial to ensuring Bagan's longevity as a cultural treasure.

Climate change adds an additional layer of concern. Rising temperatures and extreme weather events can accelerate the deterioration of ancient structures. Efforts to mitigate these impacts involve monitoring and implementing adaptive strategies to protect Bagan's architectural heritage for future generations.

Community engagement plays a vital role in Bagan's preservation efforts. Local communities are integral stakeholders in safeguarding their cultural heritage. Initiatives that promote sustainable tourism, educate residents about the importance of preservation, and provide economic incentives for conservation are key to the long-term success of preservation efforts.

Technological advancements, such as digital mapping and 3D modeling, offer innovative ways to document, study, and monitor Bagan's structures. These tools contribute to the understanding of the site's history and aid in making informed preservation decisions.

Bagan's preservation journey is a reflection of Myanmar's commitment to conserving its cultural treasures. The site's timeless beauty and spiritual significance continue to captivate the world, and efforts to balance preservation with modernization showcase the nation's dedication to preserving its history while embracing its future.

Mandalay: Cultural Heart of Myanmar

Mandalay, the second-largest city in Myanmar, occupies a special place in the nation's cultural fabric. This chapter unravels the layers of history, art, and spirituality that converge in Mandalay, making it a vibrant and cherished cultural hub that embodies Myanmar's traditions, aspirations, and artistic expressions.

Named after the mythical city in Buddhism, Mandalay was established in 1857 by King Mindon as the last royal capital of the Burmese monarchy. Its strategic location along the Irrawaddy River contributed to its significance as a trading and cultural center. The city was meticulously designed, with the Royal Palace at its center, surrounded by impressive moats and walls.

Mandalay is renowned for its artistic heritage, with traditional crafts like silk weaving, wood carving, and gold leaf making still thriving. The Mahamuni Pagoda, home to a revered Buddha image covered in layers of gold leaf, showcases the city's devotion and artistic craftsmanship. The Zaycho Market, a bustling hub, is a treasure trove of handicrafts, gems, and local goods.

The city's historic and cultural significance extends to its monasteries and temples. Shwenandaw Monastery, known for its intricate teak carvings, was originally part of the Royal Palace complex. The Kuthodaw Pagoda, often called the "World's Largest Book," houses a complex of white stupas, each containing a marble slab inscribed with Buddhist scriptures.

Mandalay's vibrant literary tradition also flourished during the Konbaung Dynasty. The city's poets, playwrights, and scholars contributed to Myanmar's literary landscape, creating works that continue to influence the nation's culture and language.

The Mandalay Hill stands as a testament to the city's spiritual significance. Pilgrims and visitors climb the hill to reach the Sutaungpyei Pagoda, where panoramic views of the city and its surroundings offer a sense of serenity and perspective. The Mandalay Palace, though partially reconstructed, still reflects the grandeur of the past and serves as a reminder of the city's royal legacy.

In modern times, Mandalay's cultural heritage remains vibrant. Traditional dance, music, and theatrical performances continue to captivate audiences, reflecting the city's role as a cultural nucleus. The Moustache Brothers, a comedy troupe known for their political satire, showcase the resilience and creativity of Mandalay's artists.

However, the city also faces challenges that accompany rapid urbanization. Infrastructure development, population growth, and environmental issues pose a delicate balance between modernization and preserving its cultural identity. Conservation efforts are being undertaken to protect the city's historic sites and ensure they remain accessible to future generations.

Mandalay's role as a cultural heart extends beyond its physical boundaries. The city's influence is felt through its music, literature, art, and traditions, which resonate throughout Myanmar. The annual Mandalay Cultural Festival showcases the city's diversity and serves as a platform for cultural exchange and celebration.

Yangon: Gateway to the Past and Present

Yangon, the largest city and former capital of Myanmar, is a city of contrasts that bridges the gap between tradition and modernity. This chapter takes you on a journey through Yangon's rich historical tapestry, its architectural marvels, and its role as a dynamic urban center that encapsulates Myanmar's evolution from the past to the present.

Founded as a small fishing village by the British in 1852, Yangon's strategic location along the Irrawaddy River delta soon transformed it into a bustling trading port. Under British colonial rule, Yangon became a key administrative and economic center, marked by the grandeur of colonial-era architecture that still graces the city.

The iconic Shwedagon Pagoda, believed to be over 2,600 years old, stands as a beacon of spirituality and a testament to Yangon's historical significance. This gilded stupa, with its towering spire and elaborate ornaments, attracts pilgrims, devotees, and visitors from around the world. The pagoda is often bathed in golden light during sunset, creating a mesmerizing spectacle.

Colonial-era architecture shapes much of Yangon's cityscape, with elegant buildings reflecting a blend of British, Burmese, and Indian influences. The Strand Hotel, built in 1901, evokes the city's colonial past and serves as a historical landmark. The Yangon City Hall, designed by Burmese architect U Tin, showcases a fusion of traditional and European architectural styles.

The Bogyoke Aung San Market, also known as Scott Market, offers a glimpse into Yangon's vibrant market culture. The market, named after the father of modern Myanmar, Bogyoke Aung San, is a labyrinth of shops selling everything from traditional handicrafts to modern fashion.

Yangon's role as a cultural hub is evident in its diverse neighborhoods. The Chinatown district pulses with energy, offering a kaleidoscope of flavors, markets, and religious sites. The Little India area reflects the city's multicultural fabric, with colorful temples, bustling streets, and aromatic spices.

The city's recent transformation is equally compelling. The opening of the country in the 21st century marked a new era of change for Yangon. Economic reforms and increased foreign investment have led to a wave of modernization, transforming the skyline with high-rises and commercial developments.

The Sule Pagoda, situated in the heart of Yangon, serves as a focal point for both spiritual and political gatherings. It was a central location during the pro-democracy protests in the late 20th century, reflecting the city's role as a stage for activism and change.

As Yangon grows, it grapples with the challenges of preserving its historical legacy while embracing modernity. Conservation efforts strive to protect colonial architecture and heritage sites amidst the rapid development. The Yangon Heritage Trust plays a crucial role in advocating for the preservation of the city's historical structures.

Yangon's allure lies not just in its architecture and history, but in the resilience and vibrancy of its people. Its dynamic street food culture, art scene, and diverse communities mirror the nation's multi-ethnic identity and spirit.

In Yangon, the past and present converge in a symphony of culture, architecture, and human interaction. The city's evolution serves as a microcosm of Myanmar's journey, reflecting its complex tapestry of traditions, aspirations, and the inexorable march of progress. As Yangon embraces the future, it remains anchored in its heritage, inviting travelers to step into a city that bridges time and tells a story of a nation in transformation.

Inle Lake and Traditional Living

Nestled amidst the Shan Hills in eastern Myanmar, Inle Lake stands as a captivating oasis of natural beauty and cultural significance. This chapter delves into the unique way of life that thrives around the lake's tranquil waters, where traditional living, intricate fishing techniques, and vibrant markets create a tapestry of living heritage.

Inle Lake stretches across 116 square kilometers, surrounded by lush mountains and floating gardens. It is home to several ethnic groups, including the Intha people, who have crafted an exceptional way of life intertwined with the lake's rhythms. The Intha are known for their distinct rowing technique, standing on one leg while propelling their wooden boats with the other.

The lake's iconic stilted villages capture the essence of traditional living. Houses, temples, and workshops are perched above the water on sturdy bamboo stilts, creating a harmonious blend of land and water. The waterways serve as roads, and boat travel is an essential means of transportation and communication.

One of the most intriguing aspects of life on Inle Lake is its floating gardens. The Intha people ingeniously cultivate crops on vast expanses of floating vegetation, primarily using water hyacinths and lake muck. These gardens yield tomatoes, cucumbers, and other produce, showcasing the ingenuity of adapting to the lake's unique environment.

The Phaung Daw Oo Pagoda, nestled along the lake's shores, is a spiritual and cultural epicenter. The pagoda enshrines five gilded Buddha images, which are carried around the lake during the annual Phaung Daw Oo Festival. This event draws thousands of devotees and visitors who witness the spectacle of traditional boat races and vibrant celebrations.

The lake's weekly markets are a testament to its role as a trading hub. The rotating markets give local communities an opportunity to buy, sell, and trade goods, from fresh produce to handicrafts. The Ywama Market, floating on the lake's surface, is a colorful spectacle that offers insights into the daily lives of the lake's residents.

In recent years, Inle Lake's popularity as a tourist destination has grown, attracting visitors intrigued by its unique lifestyle and natural beauty. However, the surge in tourism has led to challenges, including waste management and environmental conservation. Responsible tourism practices are being promoted to ensure that the lake's ecosystem and traditional way of life are preserved.

Efforts to protect Inle Lake's cultural and natural heritage are ongoing. Organizations and initiatives focus on sustainable development, conservation of the lake's biodiversity, and supporting the livelihoods of local communities. These efforts aim to strike a balance between maintaining traditional practices and embracing economic opportunities.

Inle Lake's timeless charm lies in its harmonious blend of tradition and adaptation. The unique living heritage of the Intha people reflects a way of life deeply rooted in nature, culture, and spirituality. As Myanmar continues to evolve, Inle Lake serves as a reminder of the value of preserving traditional practices while embracing the benefits of progress. It is a living testament to the nation's ability to adapt, thrive, and honor its cultural heritage in the face of change.

Kyaiktiyo Pagoda and Spiritual Significance

High in the mist-shrouded mountains of Mon State, the Kyaiktiyo Pagoda stands as a symbol of Myanmar's deep spiritual connection and unwavering faith. This chapter delves into the fascinating history, awe-inspiring architecture, and profound spiritual significance that surround this gravity-defying wonder.

The Kyaiktiyo Pagoda, commonly known as the Golden Rock, defies both gravity and explanation. Perched precariously on the edge of a massive granite boulder, the pagoda appears as if it could topple over at any moment. According to legend, the boulder is balanced on a strand of Buddha's hair, making it a site of immense reverence and devotion.

The pilgrimage to the Kyaiktiyo Pagoda is an arduous journey that draws pilgrims and visitors from across Myanmar and beyond. The trail leading to the summit involves a steep ascent, often undertaken barefoot as a gesture of humility and respect. The journey itself becomes an act of devotion, echoing the spiritual quest of the faithful.

The pagoda is an intricate work of art, clad in layers of gold leaf that shimmer in the sunlight. The boulder's surface has been smoothed by generations of devotees who have pressed gold leaf onto it as an offering. This cumulative act of reverence lends the Golden Rock its distinctive appearance, a fusion of architectural beauty and spiritual devotion.

The Kyaiktiyo Pagoda Festival, held during the full moon of Tabaung (March), is a grand celebration that draws thousands of pilgrims. The pagoda's boulder is illuminated with thousands of candles, transforming the site into a shimmering beacon of light and devotion. The festival also features colorful processions, traditional performances, and offerings to the Buddha.

The spiritual significance of the Kyaiktiyo Pagoda lies in its role as a site of pilgrimage and prayer. Devotees come seeking blessings, good fortune, and spiritual fulfillment. The pagoda is a place of reflection, where visitors meditate, offer prayers, and participate in rituals that connect them to the teachings of Buddhism.

The Golden Rock is not just a religious site; it is also a testament to the enduring cultural and historical ties of Myanmar's people. Its location in the Mon State reflects the importance of indigenous traditions and the legacy of the Mon people, who have nurtured the pagoda for centuries.

However, the Kyaiktiyo Pagoda faces challenges that stem from its popularity. The increase in visitors has led to concerns about waste management and environmental impact. Conservation efforts are being undertaken to ensure that the site's natural beauty is preserved for future generations.

The Golden Rock's enigmatic allure is a testament to Myanmar's spiritual heritage, cultural resilience, and the enduring power of faith. Its gravity-defying position and the devotion it inspires encapsulate the essence of

Buddhism, offering a profound connection to both the earthly and the divine. As pilgrims continue to ascend the mountain and pay homage to the Golden Rock, the site's spiritual significance remains undiminished, a timeless beacon of devotion and reverence.

Colonial Remnants and Architectural Legacy

Myanmar's colonial history left an indelible mark on its landscape and culture, shaping the nation's architectural legacy in ways that continue to captivate and reflect its complex past. This chapter delves into the remnants of Myanmar's colonial era, the architectural heritage that endures, and the echoes of a time that remain etched in the nation's identity.

British colonial rule, which lasted from the mid-19th century until the early 20th century, introduced significant changes to Myanmar's urban and architectural landscape. The colonial authorities established administrative centers, often marked by the construction of government buildings, railways, and ports that served their economic interests.

Yangon, formerly known as Rangoon, emerged as a hub of colonial architecture. The city's grandeur was characterized by Victorian and Edwardian-era buildings that mirrored European styles. Structures such as the City Hall, General Post Office, and the High Court, constructed between the late 19th and early 20th centuries, were imposing edifices that embodied British authority.

The Strand Hotel, built in 1901, epitomizes Yangon's colonial elegance. A symbol of luxury and sophistication, it hosted luminaries such as Rudyard Kipling and Somerset Maugham. The hotel's graceful façade, teak-panelled interior, and period furniture evoke the splendor of a bygone era.

Mandalay, the last royal capital of Myanmar, also bears colonial imprints. The Mandalay Railway Station, completed in 1903, stands as an architectural gem that echoes the region's colonial past. The station's red-brick façade and clock tower harken back to a time when the railway was a pivotal link between Mandalay and Yangon.

Kalaw, a hill station established during colonial rule, is known for its charming colonial-era houses that are now hotels and guesthouses. These structures blend British architectural aesthetics with local building techniques, creating a fusion of cultures that mirrors Myanmar's colonial history.

The architectural legacy of Myanmar's colonial era reflects more than just aesthetics; it reflects the nation's complex journey towards modernization. While these buildings served the interests of the colonial authorities, they also served as venues for social and political gatherings that laid the foundation for Myanmar's nationalist movement.

The struggle for independence, led by figures like Aung San, unfolded against the backdrop of colonial architecture. Historic events such as the University Strike of 1920 and the anti-colonial protests in the 1930s were often centered around these structures. The remnants of these protests, including speeches and slogans inscribed on walls, evoke the spirit of resistance that flourished within these architectural spaces.

As Myanmar transitioned to independence in 1948, the architectural legacy of colonial rule was transformed into symbols of national identity. Some buildings were repurposed for government use, while others remained as historical landmarks. The enduring presence of these structures serves as a reminder of Myanmar's tumultuous history and its emergence as a sovereign nation.

The colonial-era architecture remains a tangible link to Myanmar's past, offering insights into its political, cultural, and social evolution. The debate over whether to preserve, repurpose, or renovate these structures reflects the complexity of reconciling historical legacy with the demands of a rapidly changing society.

The colonial remnants stand as a testament to Myanmar's resilience, adaptation, and determination to shape its own destiny. These buildings, while vestiges of a colonial past, are also part of Myanmar's present and future, embodying its rich history and the enduring spirit of a nation in transformation.

Conclusion

The journey through the history of Myanmar has been a captivating exploration of a nation that has weathered centuries of change, adaptation, and resilience. From the mythical origins and early settlers to the modern challenges and aspirations, Myanmar's story is one of complexity, diversity, and enduring spirit.

Throughout its history, Myanmar has been shaped by a confluence of cultures, ethnicities, and influences. From the Pyu, Mon, and Bamar civilizations to the colonial era and the struggles for independence, the nation's identity has evolved through a tapestry of historical events and interactions.

The ancient kingdoms, such as the Pyu and Mon, forged cultural and economic connections that left an indelible mark on the region. The emergence of powerful empires like the Bagan Dynasty and the Arakan Empire showcased Myanmar's capacity for innovation and its ability to thrive as a cultural and economic hub.

The colonial era introduced Myanmar to European influence, leaving behind a legacy of architecture, resistance, and the seeds of nationalism. The struggle for independence, led by figures like Aung San, marked a pivotal point in Myanmar's history, paving the way for self-determination and sovereignty.

The modern era, marked by political upheavals, ethnic conflicts, and the pursuit of democratic reforms, has brought Myanmar into the global spotlight. The challenges faced by the nation reflect its intricate tapestry of ethnicities, ideologies, and aspirations.

Myanmar's natural beauty, from the lush landscapes to the serene lakes, provides a backdrop to its rich cultural heritage. The spiritual significance of sites like the Shwedagon Pagoda, the Kyaiktiyo Pagoda, and the temples of Bagan serve as a testament to the nation's deep spiritual connections and the enduring power of faith.

As Myanmar navigates the path towards the future, it stands at a crossroads of tradition and modernity. The preservation of its cultural heritage, the reconciliation of its diverse ethnic groups, and the pursuit of economic development are challenges that shape its trajectory.

The story of Myanmar is a dynamic narrative, characterized by growth, transformation, and the unyielding spirit of its people. Its history is a living testament to the resilience of a nation that has faced triumphs and tribulations, often shaped by the determination of its citizens to shape their own destiny.

As we close this chapter on the history of Myanmar, we recognize that the nation's story continues to unfold, with each passing day contributing to its ever-evolving narrative. Myanmar's journey, with its complexities, contradictions, and aspirations, remains an integral part of the global tapestry of human history. It is a story that invites reflection, exploration, and an understanding of the nation's place in the world and its boundless potential for the future.

We sincerely appreciate your time and dedication in exploring the rich history of Myanmar with us. The journey through its ancient civilizations, powerful empires, colonial struggles, and modern challenges has been an illuminating experience. We hope that this book has provided you with valuable insights into the diverse cultural tapestry, the indomitable spirit of its people, and the enduring heritage that defines Myanmar.

If you found this book informative and engaging, we kindly ask for your support by leaving a positive review. Your feedback not only encourages us to continue creating quality content but also helps other readers discover the wonders of Myanmar's history. Your voice matters, and we are grateful for your time and consideration.

Thank you once again for embarking on this journey with us. We look forward to sharing more captivating narratives and explorations with you in the future.

Printed in Great Britain
by Amazon